I TRIED TO WRITE A BRILLIANT JOKE BOOK!
ONE WITH AMAZING CARTOONS.
THAT CHILDREN WOULD WANT TO READ
AGAIN AND AGAIN.
I HOPED TO THAT MY JOKE BOOK WOULD MAKE
EVEN THE MOST SERIOUS ADULT SMILE A
LITTLE AND REMEMBER THE JOYS OF CHILDHOOD.

AND IF I FAILED, OH WELL...
I HAD AWFUL LOT OF FUN TRYING!

Why are elephants so grey
and wrinkled.

Well have you ever tried
ironing one?

Hotel guest: Are the rooms here quiet?

Hotel manager: Yes, very. It's the
guests who are noisy.

Teacher: James are you feeling indecisive
again?

James: Well, yes and no.

Sister: "When you leave school you'll make a great road sweeper."

Brother: "But I don't even know how to do it."

Sister: "Don't worry you'll pick it up as you go along!"

Why was Dopey asked to leave the library?

Because he'd whistle while he worked.

What's brown and sticky?

A stick.

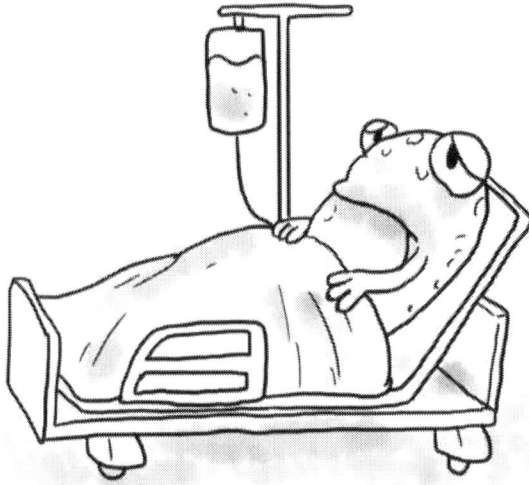

How does a frog with a broken leg feel?

Very unhoppy.

What's smelly and jumps all over Australia?

A kangapoo.

What do you get if you cross a leopard with a hippo?

A hippospotamus.

On what day should you not visit a monster?

Chewsday!

(Tuesday)

What do you sing when a
cake gets married?

"Here crumbs the bride!"

How do you cut through waves?

With a sea-saw.

How did Noah get his toilets
on the ark?

They came on loo by loo.

What jumper keeps you warm
and helps you swim?

A turtle neck sweater.

Where did Napoleon keep his armies?

Up his sleevies.

What's invisible and jumps up and
down all day in a field?

A Glasshopper.

What did the lemon say to
the orange?

Anything you can do,
I can do bitter.

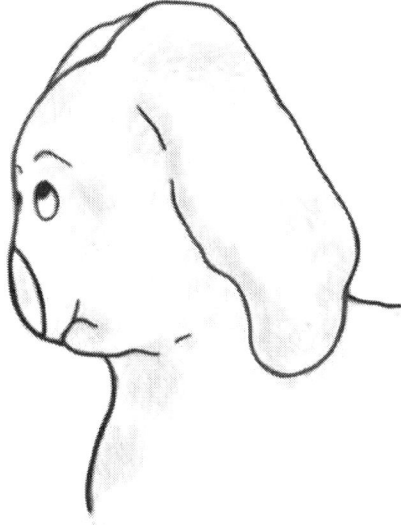

Why didn't the elephant enjoy
his holiday.

Because the airline lost his trunk.

How do you get down from
an elephant?

You don't you get down from
a duck.

What's large gray and hard
to spot?

A stain resistant elephant.

How do bees get to school?

On the school Buzz!

Why are bakers daft?

Because they sell what
they knead.

What did the policeman say
to his belly?

Don't move you're under
a vest.

What month do lazy soldiers
hate?

March.

What did the policeman say to
the snowman robbing a bank?

'FREEZE!'

Where do snowmen go to dance?

They go to snowballs.

Why are cooks cruel?

Because the batter the fish
and beat the eggs.

Why is the moon bald?

Because he eclipse it.

What would you do if a fifteen foot
monster sat in front you at the movies?

Miss most of the film!

What kind of jokes do chiropodist tell?

Corny ones.

Mum: How did your new job go
as a human cannonball?

Dad: I was fired.

Why did the clown go to
the doctors?

He felt a little funny.

What's black and white and goes up
and down?

A penguin stick in a lift.

Why are hairdressers such good drivers?

Because they know all the
short cuts.

What did the judge say to the dentist?

Do you swear, to pull the tooth
the whole tooth and nothing
but the tooth?

Where do you keep crazy balloons?

In the balloonatic asylum.

Why aren't elephants allowed
in swimming pools?

Because they keep letting their
trunks down.

Boyfriend: How could I ever leave you?

Girlfriend: By plane, train, car, bicycle.

Boyfriend: Did you miss me whilst I was
on vacation?

Girlfriend: You were on vacation?

Mom: Will you still love me when I'm
old and gray?

Dad: Of course I do darling.

Brother: That cake was lovely and
still warm, yummy!

Sister: Yes, the cats been sitting
on it all day.

Why did the one eyed monster
give up teaching?

Because he only had one pupil.

What should you do if you find
a blue monster?

Try and cheer him up.

Very Silly Signs!

All these signs are real!

Outside a chip shop:

WE FOUND NEMO.
FISH SANDWICHES
ARE BACK!

Sign in men's toilet:

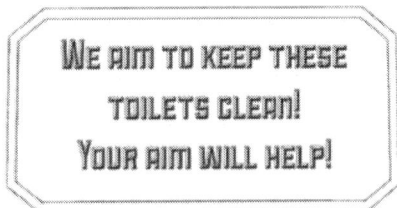

WE AIM TO KEEP THESE
TOILETS CLEAN!
YOUR AIM WILL HELP!

Sign inside a shop:

ANYONE
CAUGHT EXITING
THRU THIS DOOR
WILL BE ASKED
TO LEAVE!

Sign outside a house:

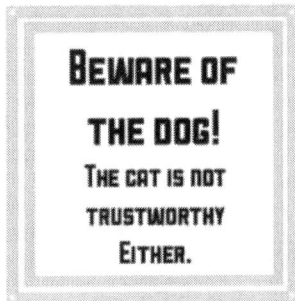

BEWARE OF
THE DOG!
THE CAT IS NOT
TRUSTWORTHY
EITHER.

Sign in delicatessen:

Our tongue
sandwiches speak
for themselves!

Outside safari:

BEWARE

WILD
ANIMALS/
CHILDREN

What time do astronauts eat?

At launch time.

Why was the musician arrested?

Because he got into treble.

How can you tell if an oceans friendly?

It waves.

What do you get if you cross
a river with a stream?

Wet.

Why was the toilet paper, rolling
down the hill?

To get to the bottom.

Why did the tide turn?

Because the seaweed.

Why was the river rich?

Because it's got two banks.

What do lonely pine trees do?

They pine.

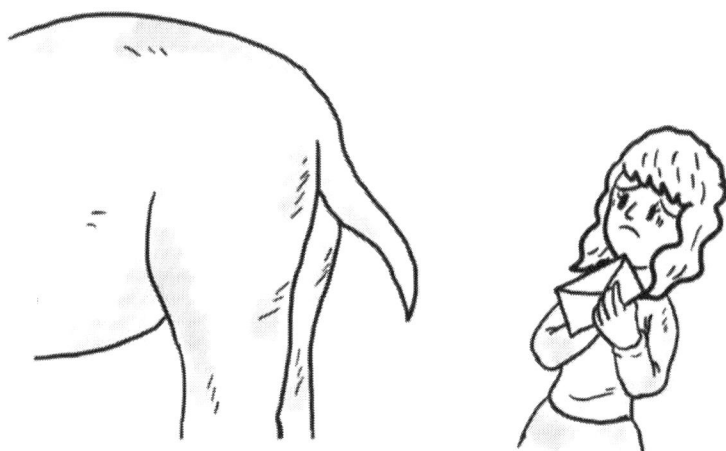

What is the difference between a letterbox and an elephant's bum?

You don't know? Remind me never to ask you to post a letter.

How do you scramble eggs?
S-g-e-g.

What's the tallest room in any school?
The library, it has so many stories.

What's the quickest way to double your money?
Fold it in half.

Dog advertisement in pet shop.

Buy one get one flea.

What do you call a smelly pirate?

Pong John Silver.

How do you spell America?

Amerrikaaa.

That's not how the dictionary spells it.

You didn't ask me how the dictionary spells it, you asked how I spell it!

How do you make fruit punch?

Put them in a boxing ring.

What did the pen say to the rubber?

Take me to your ruler.

What do you get if you order a ginormous
duck in a restaurant?

A very large bill.

What do you call a boy with
a rabbit up his jumper?

Warren.

How do you when it's been raining cats and dogs?

When you step into a poodle.

What did the fork say when he married a knife?

I'm over the spoon!

Why was the math book sad?

Because it had so many problems.

A man walked up to a policeman with a kangaroo he'd found and asked the policeman what he should do? "Take him to the zoo immediately."said the policeman. The next day the policeman saw the same man walking down the street with the same kangaroo. "I thought I told you to take him to the zoo." Said the angry policeman.
"Yes, I took him to the zoo and he liked it so much that I decided to take him to the movies today." Replied the man.

What do dragons call knights in shining armour?

Tinned food!

How do you find a bakers shop?

Head yeast!

Did Adam have a date with Eve?

No just an apple!

What time is it when you sit on a stinging nettle?

Spring time!

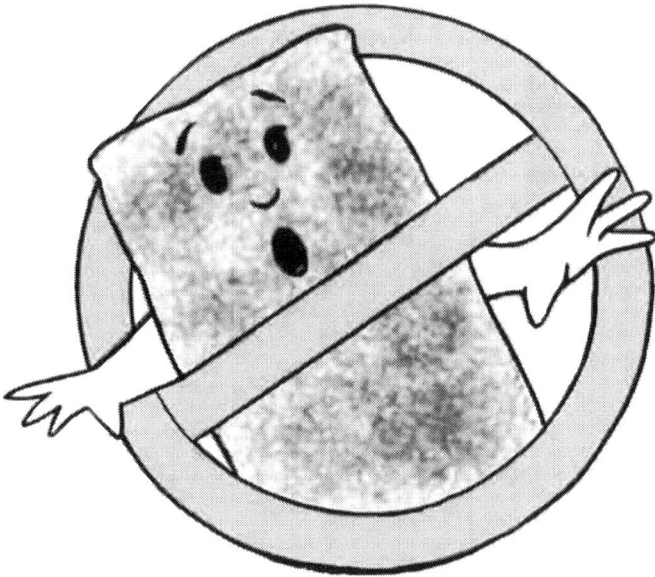

Who do you call if you've
got a spooky bread bin?

TOASTBUSTERS!

How do Eskimo children dress?

Quickly!

Teacher: What does 'coincidence' mean?
Jim: That's funny, I was going to ask you the
same thing.

What happens if you eat uranium?

You get atomic-ache.

Why are ducks early risers?

Because they get up at the quack of dawn!

Patient to brain surgeon:
"If you mess this operation up you'll get a piece of my mind!"

Why did the atom cross the road?

It was time to split.

What drink do astronauts miss most whilst in space?

Gravi-tea.
(Gravity)

What do you give a sick
monster?

Plenty of room!

Why did the scientist blow up
his doorbell?

Because he wanted to win
the Nobel prize.

What's the hardest thing about
learning to sky dive?

The ground.

Why was the chicken asked to
leave the classroom?

For using Fowl language.

Who gives puppies Christmas
presents?

Santa paws.

How long does it take to learn
ice hockey?

About a hundred sittings.

How can you swim half
a mile in 20 seconds?

Swim over a waterfall.

Why was Dracula so depressed.

He loved in vein.

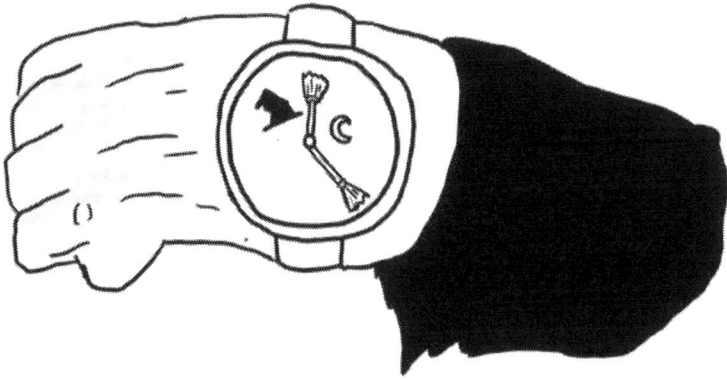

How do witches tell the time?

With a witch watch.

Why was Dracula thrown out
of art school?

He could only draw blood.

What do you call a warm sunny day
following two rainy days?

Monday.

What kind of key opens a banana?

A monkey?

Why did the pony cough?

He was a little hoarse.

Why did the boy sleep on a
pillow of cotton candy?

He wanted to have sweet
dreams!

What did boy candle say to
girl candle?

Will you go out with me?

Why did the boy candle
split up with the girl candle?

They had a heated argument,
and she got on his wick.

What do you get every birthday?

A year older.

Why did the man sleep under
his car?

Because he had to get up
oily for work.

Jim: I get heartburn every time
I eat birthday cake.
Sue: Take off the candles next time.

What do you call an adult balloon?

A blown up.

What should you do if your
nose goes on strike?

Picket!

What do you call a man stuck
halfway up a chimney in December?

Santa-pause.

Sarah: Do you ever file your nails?
Sue: Yuck! No, I just bin mine.

Dad: I've just swallowed a bone.
Son: Are you chocking?
Dad: No, I'm serious!

Son: How old can you live
without a brain?
Dad: Well, how old are you son?

Tongue Twister! 100 points.
Tenderly tickled teapots trickle terrific tea.

What do you get if you cross a
dog with a telephone?

A golden receiver.

What do you get if someone
hits you over the head with an axe?

A splitting headache.

Why did the bees go on strike?

Because they wanted more honey
and shorter working flowers!

What do you call a dinosaur who
won't stop talking about himself.

A dinobore.

Why did the dinosaur take a shower?

To become ex-stinked.

What followed the dinosaurs?

Their tails.

Why did the man only eat twigs,
leaves and the odd rusty can?

He was a hedge-tarian.

(Vegetarian)

Son: Dad can you help me with
my homework?
Dad: It wouldn't be right son.
Son: Yes, I'll ask mum instead.

Why did the cookie go to the doctors?

Because he was feeling a little crumby.

Sue: Dad how old are you?
Dad: I'm 35, but I don't look it, do I?
Sue: No, but you used to.

Sue: You're wearing my school Jumper.
Jim: No, I'm not. Yours is the one I dropped down the loo.

Son: Mum, you know you've been constantly worrying that I'll fail history?
Mum: Yes?
Son: Well, your worries are over.

(Tongue Twister 300 points)

Greedy grinning goblins grab ginormous grubs.

Knock, knock.
Who's there?
Felix.
Felix who?
Felix my ice cream again, I'll thump him.

Knock, knock.
Who's there?
Arch.
Arch who?
Sounds like you caught a cold.

Knock, knock.
Who's there.
Lucy.
Lucy who.
Lucy lastic. My pants are falling down.

Knock, knock.
Who's there?
Eve.
Eve who?
Eve ho my hearties!

Knock, knock.
Who's there?
Donut.
Donut who?
Donut open until Christmas.

Knock, knock.
Who's there?
Chimney.
Chimney who?
Chimney criket! Have you seen Pinocchio?

Strange Library

Coffee maker
by Phil Turr

REMEMBERING ANNIVERSARIES
BY BETTY WONT

Great Breakfast
By Hammond Deggs

Bull Fighting
by Matt Adore

Leaky Boat
By I . C. King

Building Wigwams
By T. P

Long Winter
By Ron. E. Nose

Lovely Breakfast
by Roland Jam

How to keep pigs
By Chris p. Bacon

LIFE IN PRISON
BY ROBBIN BANKS

OLD SCHOOL RECORDING
BY CASS ETE

Blushing
By Rosie Cheeks

Antibiotics
By Penny Silling

Nosey neighbours
by Annette Curtain

Very Silly Signs!

All these signs are real!

Sign outside office:

ATTENTION

THE FIFTH FLOOR HAS TEMPORARILY BEEN MOVED TO THE SEVENTH FLOOR!

Sign outside shop:

Come in
We're
CLOSED

Sign outside a hotel:

FREE WI-FI

STARTING AT
€59 DOLLARS

Sign inside a park:

No signs Allowed!

Sign down a street:

KEEP
←
RIGHT

Sign outside flats:

Warning!

Bicycles chained to these railings will be moved without notice
THIS IS A NOTICE!

How do you know when a twenty
foot monsters under your bed?
Your nose touches the ceiling.

Why was tiger looking down the
toilet?
He was looking for Pooh.

What do you call an underwater spy?
James Pond. (bubble 07)

Why did the jelly wobble?
Because it saw the milkshake.

How do you make a jacket potato
look smart?
With button mushrooms.

What do you get if you cross
a sausage with a car?
An old banger!

What biscuit can fly?
A plane one.

How do you make an apple puff?
Chase it around the kitchen.

How do you make an apple turnover?
Push it off the table.

How do you make a turkey stew?
Keep it waiting for hours!

What do you get if you cross an
elephant with an airplane?

A Dumbo-jet.

How do we know carrots are good
for your eyesight?

Have you ever seen a
rabbit wearing glasses?

1st egg: I'm dreading going into
that pan of boiling water.
2nd egg: That's nothing we get
beaten on the head after.

How do you tease fruit?

Banananananana!

What's the difference between an elephant and a biscuit?

Have you ever tried dunking an elephant into a cup of tea?

Why was the mushroom so popular?

Because he was a fun guy.

Why do the French eat snails?

Because they don't like fast food.

What happens if you sit on a grape?

It gives a little whine.

Why did the girl put money in her fridge?
Because she wanted cold, hard cash!

What do cornflakes wear on their feet?
Kelloggs.

Why shouldn't you tell a secret
at the greengrocers?
Because the corn has ears and
the potatoes have eyes.

How do you make a banana split?
Cut it in half.

How does Santa know when
Christmas is near?

He checks his calen-deer.

How does a hamburger propose?

With a onion ring.

What makes the Tower of Pisa Lean?

It doesn't over eat.

What's in the middle of Paris?

The letter R.

What city holds the worst singers?

Singapore.

What do you get if you cross a stream
with a river?

Wet!

What European countries should meet
for Christmas dinner?

Hungary and Turkey.

What happened to the girl who
drank 9 cans of cola?

She bought 7 up.

What's brown and sounds like a bell?

Dung!

What's invisible and smells like carrots?

Rabbit Trumps.

What do you call a hippo that
won't tidy his room?

A hippospotamess.

Why did Henry the VIII have so many wifes?

He liked to chop and change.

What do you get if you cross the Atlantic
with the Titanic.

About halfway.

What did the princess say to the
lazy knight?

Don't just sit there, slay something.

Why shouldn't you stand on a
cats tail?
It hurts it's felines.

What's green, misty and croaks?

Kermit the fog.

What's E.T short for?
He has little legs.

What's blue and smells like red paint?

Blue paint.

What kind of ape can you find at
the bottom of the sea?

A shrimpanzee.

Where do snowmen go to dance?
Snowballs!

Who's like a female sheep around here?

Ewe.

What do you get if you pour a bottle of vinegar over a T. Rex.

A Dino-sour.

Why did the baker stop making bagels?

He got tired of the whole thing.

In which country do you not need a fridge?

Chile.

Where does a 10 ft gorilla sit in a restaurant?

Anywhere he wants.

How does Tarzan clean his windows?

With a windscreen viper.

What's the best side of a house to put
the bath in?

The inside.

How can a large cook win a race?

By beating an egg.

Why was the pita bread laughing?

He had a good sense of hummus.

Because I wouldn't marry him
he made me walk the plank.
"I'll love you till the day you die."
He pushed and then I sank.

Did you here about the chicken that
laid twins?

They looked eggactly the same.

Teacher: When was the sausage invented?
Jim: Was it on a Fry-day?

What did one eye say to the other?

Between you and me,
something smells!

Sister: My teacher said I ate my dinner
with the manners of a saint.
Brother: Perhaps she meant a St. Bernard.

Can February March?

No, but April May!

I once knew a Prince too small
Who loved a princess too tall
He grew sadder and sadder
Until he found a ladder
And took it along to the ball

What's a frogs favourite book?

One with a hoppy ending.

Where do sick fish go?

To the doctopuss.

Why did the cow cross the road?
Because the grass is always
greener on the other side.

What grows bigger the more you take away?
A hole.

How many skunks does it make to a stink?

A phew.

What do you call a bee who has had a
spell put on him.

He's bee-witched.

Where do astronauts leave their spaceships?

At parking meteors.

What's wrong with a man with jelly in one ear
and sponge cake in the other?

He's a trifle deaf.

What kind of clothes can you make from
tea bags?

Baggy t-shirts.

What's yellow and stupid?

Thick custard.

What does a monster read it's children in bed?

Fright time stories.

Do cows cheat in tests?

Yes they copy each udder.

What happens if you leave bones on a sun lounger?

You get a skele-tan.

Why did captain hook cross the road?

To get to the second hand shop.

Did you hear about the chocolate factory?

It melted.

How much did the pirate pay for his peg and hook?

An arm and a leg.

Where did the snowman meet his wife?

On the winternet.

Who invented the first rain coat?

Anna Rack.

What do cats call mice?
Delicious!

Why did the elephant leave
the circus?
Because he was tired of
working for peanuts!

Did you hear about the
cow that ate only dynamite.

It ended in udder disaster!

Knock, knock.
Who's there?
Handsome.
Handsome who?
Handsome cake through the letterbox.

Knock, knock.
Who's there?
Pasture.
Pasture who?
Pasture bedtime, isn't it.

Knock, knock.
Who's there?
Little old lady.
Little old lady who?
I didn't know you could yodel.

Knock, knock.
Who's there?
Emma.
Emma who?
Emma bit cold out here, let me in!

Knock, knock.
Who's there?
Spiderman.
Spiderman who?
You mean there's more than one.

Knock, knock.
Who's there?
Iona.
Iona who?
Iona have eyes for you!

Knock, knock.
Who's there?
Louis.
Louis who?
Louis the opposite of high.

Knock, knock.
Who's there?
Hannah.
Hannah who
Hannah partridge in a pear tree!

Knock, knock.
Cook.
Cook who?
Have you been eating bird seed?

Knock, knock.
Who's there?
Omar?
Omar who?
Omar goodness! Wrong door!

Knock, knock.
Who's there?
Sonia.
Sonia who?
Sonia shoe, and it stinks!

Knock, knock.
Who's there?
Carrie.
Carrie who?
Carrie me into your house, I've broken my legs!

Knock, knock.
Who's there?
Kanga.
Kanga who?
No it's a kangaroo.

Knock, knock.
Who's there?
Twitter.
Twitter who.
Have you got an owl in there?

Knock, knock.
Who's there?
Irish stew.
Irish stew who?
Irish stew in the name of the law!

Knock, knock.
Who's there?
Walter.
Walter who?
Walter wall carpets.

Knock, knock.
Who's there?
Idapp.
Idapp who?
Yuck, too much information.

Knock, knock.
Who's there?
The doorbell repair man.

What kind of cat lives at the bottom
of the sea?

An octopussy.

Jim: I went to the doctor and he says I can't
play baseball.
Tom: Oh, did he see your last game then?

How do farmers count their cows?

With a cowculator.

What city has the most cows?

Moo York.

How did the mermaid get home from the ball?
By taxi crab.

Where did the hen meet her husband?

At a cock-a-doodle-do.

Whats yellow and has wings?
A lemon, sorry I lied about
the wings.

Son: Dad, why do you keep tapping on
my head and tickling my ears?
Dad: To keep the lions away.
Son: But there aren't any lions.
Dad: See it must be working.

What do you get if you cross a clock
with a chicken?

An alarm cluck.

How do you start a vegetable race?

Ready, steady, grow!

Why don't calculators ever break?

Because you can always count
on them.

What do frogs order at McDonald's?

French flies and croak a cola.

What animal do you look like when you take a bath?

A little bear.

What do you do if you find a spaceman?

You park in it, man.

What did the girl light bulb say to the boy light bulb?

'I love you watts, and watts..'

What was the peanut doing in hospital?

He was a salted.

Where do dogs park their cars?

In a barking lot.

(parking lot)

When was Queen Victoria buried?

Just after she died.

What kind of race is never run?

A swimming race.

What do you call a spaceship that drips water?

A crying saucer.

When do astronauts eat?

At launch time.

Why was the cow singing on stage?

She was staring in a moosical.

What do clouds wear beneath their trousers?

Thunderwear.

What do you call a relative who cleans floors?

Auntie-septic.

What should you do if your heads full of water?

Call a drain surgeon.

What noise does an exploding monkey make?

Ba-boom!

How did Vickings send secret messages?

With Norse code.
(morse code)

Who invented fire?

Some bright spark.

What did the zero say to the eight?

Nice belt.

Whats a pirates favourite lesson?
Aaaart!

Teacher: Simon can you spell your name
backwards?

Simon: No, miss.

Which queen suffered indigestion?

Queen Hic-toria.

Who's the boss of the hankies?

The Hankie-chief.

How do you keep flies out of the school canteen?
Let them taste the food.

Why is lightning badly behaved?
It doesn't know hoe to conduct itself.

What did one cloud say to the other?
I'm cirrus about you.

What athlete never gets cold?
The long jumper.

What's yellow and dangerous?

Shark infested custard.

Where do spies shop?

At the snoopermarket.

What insects can tell the time?

Clockroaches.

What grows on a wall?

A walnut.

What's purple and 4000 miles long?

The Grape wall of China.

What's the difference between a
weasel and a stoat?

A weasel is weasily recognised
but a stoat is stoatally different.

On what day do most shops sell most
bubble gum?

On Tuesdays. (Chewsdays)

Where do frogs leave their coats?

In the croakroom.

Why did the boy throw his alarm
clock out of the window?

Because he wanted to see time fly.

What kind of movie do chefs see
every day?

Cling film.

Where are sharks hiding in your bedroom?

Check your chest of jaws.

Did you hear about the beautiful women that
married a packet of self raising flour?

The locals called them Beauty and the Yeast.

How do you catch a squirrel?

Climb up a tree and act like you're nuts.

Neighbour 1: Hey, didn't you hear me? I was banging on your wall for hours last night?
Neighbour 2: No, I was playing my music too loudly.

What's at the end of everything?

G.

What's the new movie about a prehistoric pig called?

Jurassic Pork.

What cards do mice send to cats
in December?

Cross-mouse cards.

What does the salad say at church?

Lettuce pray.

Is it hard to get a greedy person to
eat more?

Nope, it's a piece of cake.

What's the recipe to make gold soup?

Just add 24 carrots.

A criminal dug a tunnel to escape from prison. The tunnel came out at a playground and he shouted I'm free, I'm free. A little girl came over to him and said I'm four.

Where do wizards kiss witches?

Under the mistle-toad.

Why did the seal cross the road?

To get to the other tide.

What can fly underwater?

A wasp in a submarine.

Where do you take a hornet with a broken wing?

To waspital.

Did you hear about the girl who slept
with her head under a pillow?

The tooth fairies came and took
all her teeth away!

Son: I took Rover to the watchmakers
Mum: Why did you that, I said take home to the vets.
Son: I thought you said he had ticks.

Why do bears have fur coats.

Well, they'd look silly in anoraks.

What's it called when a cat wins a dog show?

A cat-has-trophy!

Why did the women buy all the birds in
the pet shop?

Because the we're going cheep.

What's the difference between a french student
and an American student.

Thousands of miles.

Did you hear about the actor who fell through
the floor?

It was just a stage he was
going through.

How do you count the insects around
a lampshade?

Moth-ematics.

Knock, knock.
Who's there?
Turner.
Turner who ?
Turn around there's a monster behind you!

Knock, knock.
Who's there?
Cereal.
Cereal who?
Cereal pleasure to meet you.

Knock, knock.
Who's there?
Argue.
Argue who?
Argue going to let me in or not?

Where do cats go to when they're not working?

To the mew-seum.

Why did the crab go to prison?

He kept on pinching things.

What does father bee say after a hard days work?

Honey I'm home.

What's big green and smells?

A monsters bottom.

Knock, knock.
Who's there?
Olive.
Olive who?
Olive you so much!

Knock, knock.
Who's there?
Hawaii.
Hawaii who.
I'm fine, Hawaii you?

Knock, knock.
Who's there?
Avenue.
Avenue who?
Avenue learnt my name yet?

Oh, Did i forget to mention that this book has a family Christmas fun section hidden at the back? Well I thought it would be more fun to hide it!

The rules
Everyone must participate.
All phones and tablets must be turned off!
Just turn the page and start having
Fun!

Santa Limbo Competition!

Dad vs Kids

You must place two pillows up your jumper
before taking part. Whoever can limbo
the lowest wins 800 points.

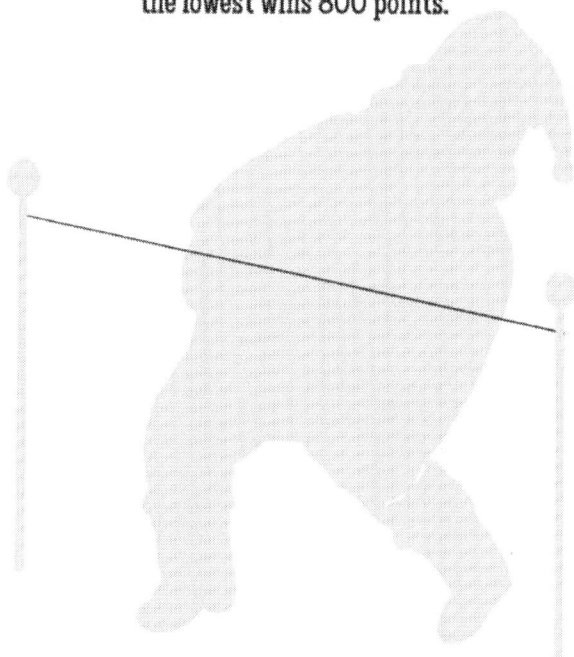

If Dad loses he has to pretend to be
a reindeer and give you reindeer rides all
around the house. If Dad refuses tell Mum!

Santa's left some invisible gifts.
Everyone has to choose a number.
Then use the invisible gift for 2 minutes
The best actor wins 500 points!

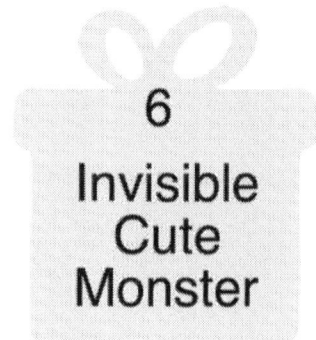

1
Invisible
Dancing
Shoes!

2
Invisible
Rocket

3
Invisible
Angry
Dinosaur

4
Invisible
Naughty
Monkey

5
Invisible
Giant
Puppy

6
Invisible
Cute
Monster

Bigger points but harder!

The best actor wins 1000 points!

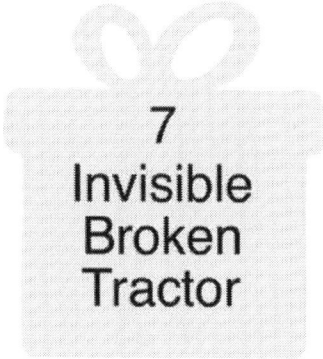

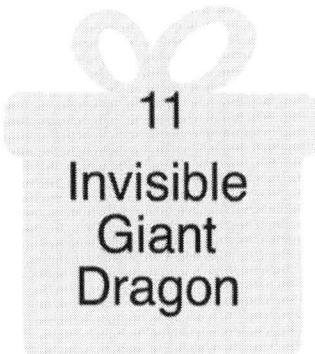

7
Invisible
Broken
Tractor

8
Invisible
Candy
Factory

9
Invisible
Dancing
Ice Skates

10
Invisible
Fight with
Batman

11
Invisible
Giant
Dragon

12
Invisible
Pirate
Ship

Dad vs Kids

Whoever can fill in left and right deer
and make them look the same wins 900 points!
Dad can only use his left hand to draw.

Kids 5 minutes
each.

Kids 5 minutes
each.

If Dad looses he has to give a reindeer ride
whilst singing a Christmas carol.

Dad 30 seconds
each.

Oh Deer Dad!

Who's next?

2 minutes
Uncle.

2 minutes
Grandma.

2 minutes
friend.

Dad vs Kids
Santa's X-ray

Get a pen and a piece of paper, you have 5 minutes to try and remember every item found in Santa's sack. The answers on the next page 70 points for every item noted.

Dad has a 30 second time limit.

X-ray Test
Test Results

Dog	Teapot
Frog	Kite
Shark	Bird
Screwdriver	Pliers
Golf club	Coat hanger
Drill	Saw
Fish	Hammer
Cat	Seahorse
Saucepan	Catapult
	Cake

Tick objects remembered!

The winners initials!

☐ ☐ ☐ ☐

☐ ☐ ☐ ☐

☐ ☐ ☐ ☐

The winners initials!

☐ ☐ ☐ ☐

☐ ☐ ☐ ☐

☐ ☐ ☐ ☐

The Grinch has hidden the C from
Christmas every adult has one
minute to find it. Children have
5 minutes each! 3000 points!

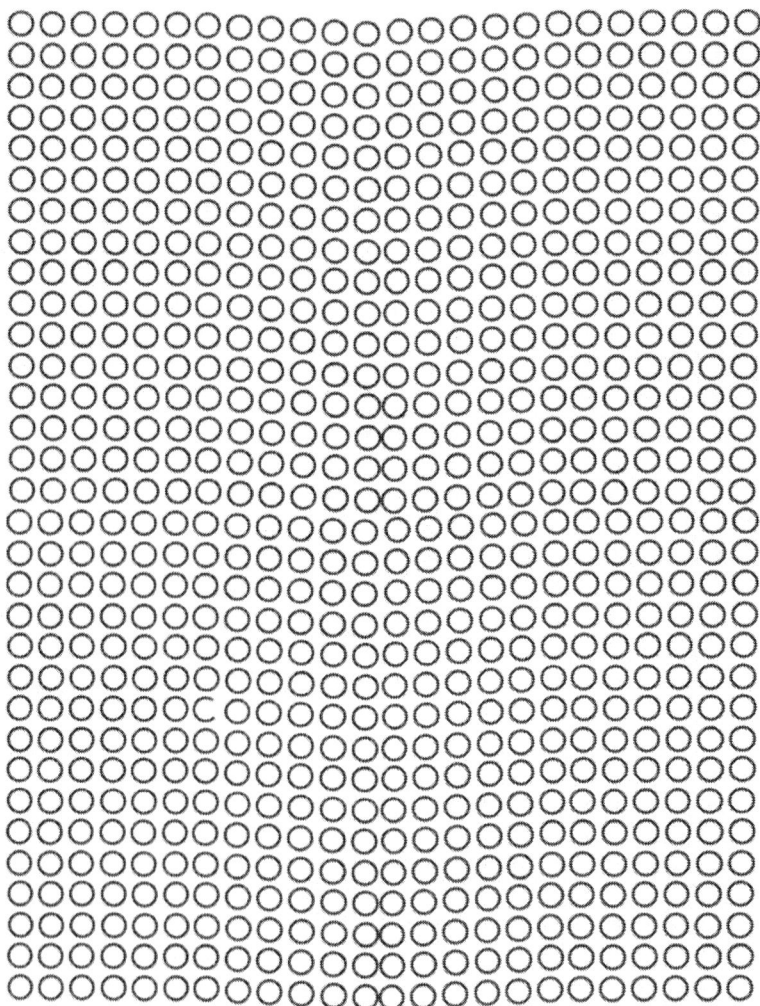

Every member of the family has to choose a stocking.
Whoever fills it with the funniest gifts wins 2000 points.

President
Trump

Elvis

Mickey
Mouse

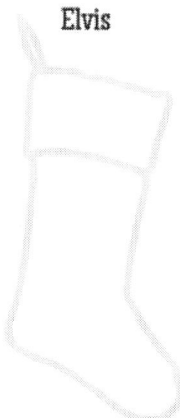

Elsa
Frozen

Snow White

The Queen

Pinocchio

R2d2

Darth Vader

Kids versus Dad!

Fill in Santa, make him look
amazing, winner wins 300 points

Kids

Kids

Kids

Dads!

You have 5 minutes to draw a funny
Grinch face then sign the image.
Funniest Grinch wins 5000 points.

Memory Test.

Poor old Santa is suffering from tinsell-itis.
Give out sheets of paper to every player
and ask them to draw this image after looking
at it for one minute for adults and 2 minutes
for children. Whoever creates the closet drawing
wins 5000 points, Moms the judge.

Now do the same with the image below
and the images on the next pages.
5000 points for every memory winner.

MERRY
CHRISTMAS

Memory Test.

5000 points.

5000 points.

Memory Test.

5000 points.

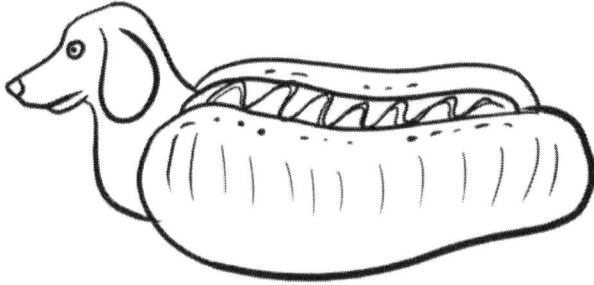

5000 points.

THANK YOU FOR PURCHASING MY
BOOK, I DO HOPE YOU LAUGHED A
LITTLE WHILST READING IT.
IF YOU ENJOYED IT PLEASE LEAVE
A REVIEW AS THIS CAN REALLY HELP SMALL
INDEPENDENT PUBLISHERS.

THANK GOD FOR
CHRISTMAS!

Young Robin

Books

Printed in the United States of America

First Printing, 2018

Contact: Sniffitysnoo302@gmail.com

Nehemiah 8:10

Printed in Great Britain
by Amazon